A Woman's Guide To Freedom

Not Just a Book, but a Personal Ministry Guide Designed
to Set You Free from Toxic, Destructive Relationships with Men!

Kathleen Steele Tolleson

Copyright © 2013 Kathleen Steele Tolleson

All rights reserved.

ISBN: 1493658301
ISBN-13: 978-1493658305

Isaiah 52: 1-2

Awake, Awake!
Put on your strength, O Zion;
Put on your beautiful garments,
O Jerusalem, the holy city!
For the uncircumcised and the unclean
Shall no longer come to you.
Shake yourself from the dust,
arise;
Loose yourself from the bonds of your neck,
O captive daughter of Zion.

KATHLEEN STEELE TOLLESON

CONTENTS

	Introduction	9
1	O CAPTIVE DAUGHTER OF ZION	11
2	SHAKE YOURSELF FROM THE DUST	21
3	LOOSE YOURSELF FROM THE BONDS	27
4	YOU HAVE SOLD YOURSELF FOR NOTHING	37
5	TOUCH NO UNCLEAN THING	43
6	PUT ON YOUR BEAUTIFUL GARMENTS	49
7	BEHOLD, IT IS I	53
8	BREAK FORTH INTO JOY	59

DEDICATION

This book is dedicated to all of the women who read the manuscript and gave me support, encouragement and feedback. And to all the women who will read it and choose to live their lives as "Daughters of a King."

THANK YOU

I would like to especially thank my husband, Rodney. God has used him to encourage and support me into destiny. I remember one day when the Lord spoke to me and said, "I have sent this man to help restore your soul, why won't you let him?" He went on to say, "Your soul was damaged by the hands of men and I have chosen this man to help bring healing and restoration."

Even though we were already married and had a good marriage, I knew God was dealing with those parts of my heart that were still somewhat guarded. I couldn't let myself need him too much. A good analogy is when you are holding a child. They might let you hold them yet they are still a bit braced but then there's that point when their whole bodies relax. I knew God wanted me to rest in the love my husband had for me. I want to thank you for holding me until I could.

And Brenda, thank you for your faithfulness, your loving me through warfare, your computer knowledge and for late hours. You know how important you are to me and I appreciate all that you do, especially those things that no one else even sees or knows about but that helps me to do what God has called me to do.

I also want to thank my family and my church family for releasing me to counsel, write, and travel when necessary. I know sometimes it is a sacrifice for all of us but I believe you too have an investment in every life that is transformed, every family that is healed, and every marriage that is restored. Thank you.

And I would be amiss, if I left out Christian International. If it weren't for Bishop Hamon and Evelyn and their vision to empower women in the Body of Christ, I would not be the woman I am today. I also want to thank our pastors, Dr. Jim and Jeanni Davis, our overseers with the Christian International Network of Churches. They are always there to nurture, share their wisdom and just love you. Thank you for believing in me.

The three most important women in my life are my mother and two daughters. They also had the challenges and opportunity to travel with me in my journey from bondage to freedom. I felt it would be appropriate to ask them to share in the Foreword of this book.

FOREWORD

I happened to be with my mom when she started this book. We were riding in the car together and she was working on her laptop and sharing as she wrote. I remember thinking how similar parts of our lives had been; with our rebellion, pride, and destructive choices. But thank God for His awesome mercy.

Now, I look up to my mom immensely. She is my favorite preacher. The way she lives her life and the way she touches the lives of others is the way I can only pray that I will be one day. She is an amazing woman, my mom. Thank you, Lord, for her. - *Leanne Kaplan*

When they speak of transformation, my mother, Kathy, is a prime example that it *is* real. God is ready to transform each one of us. I have seen her in the fullness of her old man, which was anger, strife, rebellion, and the inability to give unconditional love. I have seen her in situations that a child should never see their mother in.

Then through her, God showed me what a righteous woman was and what a Godly mother was. I am excited for the first time in my life to claim her proudly as my Mom, one that I respect and adore for the woman God created. - *Tara Romeo*

As my daughter, I witnessed the phases Kathy went through. Some were very painful to watch. But then, I saw the transformation that came about after she let God into her life. Kathy Tolleson is my daughter, my counselor, my pastor and my friend. Can I say more? - *Doris Tomljenovich*

We all recommend this book, we know that if it worked for her, it surely can work for anybody! God's power is real, His Word is true, and His mercies are new every morning. We encourage you to reach out and take hold of the new beginning God has for your life.

Introduction

This book was written for several purposes, first of all for the individual women who need ministry; women who are in destructive relationships now or those who need to prevent a reoccurrence. I tried to write it as if I was sitting in a counseling room and ministering one on one. I encourage you to take your time as you go through it.

Some women review the book initially but then go back and walk through each ministry step, slowly. Others just take their time and go step by step from the beginning. Find out what works for you. You may find it emotionally draining and even feel very tired. Sometimes, you may feel like you just have to stop before you can go any further. All of those things are very normal and are a part of facing and dealing with emotional pain. Please allow time for the Lord to minister you. It is only by His Spirit that true transformation and change takes place. I also encourage you to use the personal ministry journal space that is included. It will enhance the journey and be something that will be very precious to you in the future.

The second purpose for writing the book was for counselors, pastors and other ministers. It is an equipping tool which can help walk someone to victory over toxic, destructive relationships. I also wanted to sound an alarm in the Body of Christ because of the women falling back into relationships of bondage and victimization. As leaders, we may feel helpless to stop it. I am hoping that ministers and counselors will arm themselves with this weapon and when they see those living in toxic relationships or those going back into one, they will hand them this book. It also has been a great time-saver for me and I know it can be for other counselors and pastors, as well. Sometimes having an outside voice speaking the very same thing helps an individual to take notice of what is being said. I know I would have done anything to stop some of the women I loved and pastored from going back to destructive relationships.

The third purpose was as a tool to use for support groups. A facilitator can take a group through each section, allowing for ministry, sharing and testimonies as they go. It allows the group to have a common focus with a place to start and end. I would allow a minimum of 12 weeks to cover the information. The facilitator needs to be able to identify with the women in the group but should be in a place of victory in her own life. It was published in a workbook form so that it can be used in workshops, support groups and so women will not just read it but take the entire journey.

In the book, I share some personal information but I did not want the focus to be on me. In case you are wondering why I didn't share more, it is because this is not a book about my life. It's a book for your life. I did not want you to be thinking about what I went through or what my children went through, I want you concentrating on your life, the changes you need to make, and what God wants to do for your family. I feel honored to co labor with the Holy Spirit as He takes you on this journey. The New King James version of the Bible was used for all scripture references

Chapter 1

O Captive Daughter Of Zion

> **Isaiah 52:1-2** *"Awake, Awake! Put on your strength, O Zion; Put on your beautiful garments, O Jerusalem, the holy city!*
> *For the uncircumcised and the unclean shall no longer come to you.*
> *Shake yourself from the dust, Arise; Loose yourself from the bonds of your neck,*
> *O captive daughter of Zion.*

Women deceived – women abused – women violated – women seduced – and women who will go right back and do it again, women helpless to stop the abusive and destructive cycles in their lives. How do you help them? How do they help themselves?

The sad thing about this is that these women are Christians, women who know the Lord, yet somehow they have still not been able to appropriate the power of God in this area of their lives.

This past week was almost too much – as pastors and as Christian counselors, my husband and I are always dealing with these issues, but this week was enough to drive me to my lap top. If I can help share in some way anything that could stop another woman from continuing in these destructive cycles, I want to do it. Some of the things I share may sound a little strong, but from what I have experienced it takes a strong stand to break the power of the enemy in this area. The Bible paints a graphic picture in Proverbs 26:11 *"As a dog returns to his own vomit, so a fool repeats his folly."* Not a pretty picture is it?

Yet, we see it all the time. And last week, I saw it in abundance. And I have to be honest, even as I write this I'm wondering, *"Can it do any good? Will it do any good? Could one of these women heading on this path of destruction be persuaded to turn from the vomit?"* There have been times when they have clearly agreed with us – *"It looks like vomit, it smells like vomit, it is vomit and I don't want to go back to it."* Yet the next phone call we get is saying, *"I am back in the vomit, but I believe it will be different this time."* I've got news for you ladies, vomit is vomit, and the only way things will change is by not going back, but by going forward

I want to help the ones that have never been in the vomit to avoid it and I want to help the ones who have been in it not return back to it. I also want to reach out to the ones who have already returned to it so that they can wake up and smell it. But let's first put a definition on the vomit I'm talking about: those destructive, toxic relationships with men that leave women violated, abused, obsessed; their dignity and self-worth totally destroyed and children left in the wake of constant emotional turmoil; a home that is a war zone rather than a place of safety and refuge.

Before I became a Christian, I lived in my own share of vomit and put my two daughters through trauma, fear, and emotional upheaval. They continue to walk through their own recovery with the Lord. The only thing different from myself and the women returning to vomit was that when I became a Christian, I was able to see my sickness and by the grace of God put a stop to those toxic patterns. I know that most of the time without the power of God working in our lives, we are powerless to put an end to our self-destructive lifestyle. My real concern is for the ones who now know the Lord yet still continue living in bondage in their relationships. Beloved, that should not be.

Please understand I am not in any way advocating divorce. If you are in an unhealthy relationship, I believe you can overcome in the midst of it. I believe the Word which says your husband can be won through your conduct (1 Peter 3:1). I am advocating very strongly that if you are not married and have had a past pattern of destructive relationships that you read this book in entirety and allow the changes that must take place in you before entering into another relationship. I also believe that whenever your personal safety or health or your children's are at stake, separation may be necessary until God has an opportunity to work in your husband's life. Separation should be approached with much prayer and should be in consensus with your church leadership.

GOOD NIGHT, ANGEL

I have been very happily married for a number of years to a wonderful loving husband who still goes to bed at night and says, *"Good night, Angel."* What changed? From getting pregnant at 17, to a volatile, alcohol-driven marriage where I was called anything but Angel, to an affair, to divorce, to contracting herpes (which God so lovingly healed me from), to being in a physically abusive relationship which turned into a life threatening stalking situation, my relationships went from bad to worse. It was obvious I did not have a good track record in my choice of men. (I want to make it clear that I am not blaming these men nor do I hold any unforgiveness towards them.

I was just as responsible for the destructiveness of our relationships as they were. God has forgiven me and I have forgiven them. But why did I go from one destructive relationship to another? From alcoholic to alcoholic? From one emotionally immature man to another? From one angry man to an even angrier one.

God spoke to me one day not long after I was saved and told me "why". Now my WHY may not be your WHY. But what I am here to tell you is that there is a WHY you keep going back to your bondage, and if you want to be healed, God will show you your WHY and set you free from it. Let me tell you about mine. The Lord spoke to me that day very clearly. I could still take you back to the exact spot. He showed me the root of my sickness. He spoke to me very gently, and said *"Kathy, you're still trying to win."* And as He spoke those words I was flooded with understanding. God showed me my father who always had trouble communicating and showing emotion. I saw myself as a little girl trying to get this man to communicate as a way of demonstrating his love. I wanted my father to quit drinking and quit working long enough to pay attention to me.

Before I go on, I want to share that as the Lord healed me from my childhood pain, my relationship with my father became very close. I could see a great deal of things my father had instilled in me, a sense of adventure, a work ethic, integrity, and a knowledge that being a woman did not have to be a limiting factor in my life. He was never physically or verbally abusive. He just didn't communicate. My dad had stopped drinking in his later years and was a member of our church before he passed away. I thank God that after his death, I did not have to wrestle with the demons of unforgiveness and guilt. I knew that he had given me his best even though as a child it hadn't always felt good enough. When I look back at how much this one man affected my life just because he didn't know how to hug and wasn't much of a talker unless he was drinking, I can only imagine how difficult it must be for those who never had a father or had one that was abusive.

As the Lord shared with me that day through the spirit of counsel and understanding (Isaiah 11:2), I began to see my pattern. I had to find a man who had an alcohol problem who would quit drinking *for me*: it had to be someone who had difficulty showing emotion and communicating. The great hook was always when they said, "I've never been able to open up like this to anyone else before." God showed me the men who had shown interest in me that were gentle and good communicators and how I wouldn't have even give them the time of day. They were no challenge. I could not work out my childhood need to win in an unwinnable situation with a man that was too easy.

That day the Lord showed me that the very thing I really needed to help me in my healing was a man who could communicate with me easily and one that could freely share his feelings emotionally and physically. Yet it was the very thing that held no appeal to me. Suddenly I saw the sickness in all of it and cried out to God for my healing. The Lord showed me that my only way out was to forgive my father for what he hadn't given me and to cut my losses.

It was no longer up to me to try to work out this emotional situation with different faces, yet the same similarities. I had to give it to God and I did. I forgave my father and immediately was flooded with a sense of freedom. My heart was changed and I never returned to the vomit of a destructive relationship.

My husband is a gentle man who has never had an alcohol problem. He freely communicates his love for me. We work together as a team in business and ministry, and without a doubt he is my best friend. It's sad to say, but I know that in the days before my healing, he would have never appealed to me. Without my desires becoming healed and sanctified, I would have continually sought after that which only made the wounds deeper rather than that which would bring healing and restoration to my soul. As each wound got deeper, I somehow found a man in an even worse condition to somehow win the emotional battle I was in, even though I was totally unaware of it.

The interesting thing was that if anyone had tried to tell me that these men were like my father, I would have pointed out countless differences and told them they didn't know what they were talking about. And they were different in many ways, some more violent, some with less integrity, some different physically. But that wasn't what was important, it was where they were the same that was affecting my life, and that's what I couldn't see on my own. It took the eyes of the Lord to give me insight and understanding that set me free.

SOUL BATTLES

I call this need of the soul to "win" soul battles. It is the need of the soul to recreate situations that we have felt defeated in as children. I needed to win in the battle to change my father into a communicative, affectionate man who did not drink. Time ran out on me. I grew up. But my soul had not given up. It continued to draw those type of circumstances to me which always ended up totally self-defeating.

Soul battles can take many different shapes and forms. I could give you countless scenarios but will only share a few as examples. The Holy Spirit is faithful and will show you where your soul has been locked in battle. As you give it up and admit defeat, you will feel great rest come into your spirit and soul. It gives whole new meaning to the Scripture; *The battle is the Lord's,* 2 Chronicles 20:15. When our carnal nature tries to produce successful results in our life, we are set up for failure.

Let me share a couple of different examples. One that comes to mind was a young man whose mother was always depressed and melancholy. As he was growing up, this son decided in his heart that he would be so funny and good that one day his mom would get happy. However, once again, time ran out on him and he lost the battle. His mother fought depression all of her life. However, his soul transferred the battle to other women and guess who he married. You got it - a woman who had problems with depression.

Where did their marriage have problems? Basically they surrounded his attempt to control and try to "lovingly" force her to become the happy woman he always wanted and needed. Once he saw the battle and released his need and his wife to the Lord, she was finally free to receive healing and ministry. Once we give up the soul battle, our prayers become even more effective. Even though he had been saying all along, "Lord give her joy, change her into a happy woman'" his soul still wanted to be the one who finally accomplished the mission.

Another example that comes to mind was the businessman who had been divorced several times and he tended to have clients with a certain life pattern. The women including his own wives and the wives of his clients tended to be negative, critical, and against any entrepreneurial activities. The men he ended up consulting with all tended to be passive, hated the control of the woman, but ultimately couldn't stand up for themselves and would cave in to their wives pressure. When we uncovered the soul battle, it was in his need to save his father from a premature death. He lost but his soul was continually trying to recreate the situation. His own father had died torn between pursuing his dreams and giving into the negative fears of his wife. This businessman was continually trying to get the men, including himself, to rise up against the negative control of their wives while at the same time trying to change the women into supportive, encouraging and positive wives. Over and over again, he lost. He was able to finally recognize and receive ministry from the soul battle. Through freedom, he now has a happy marriage and is no longer recreating the scenario over and over again in his professional life.

Sound strange? Can the soul really exercise that much power? I assure you it does. That is why we must build up our spirit man so our spirit can deal with our soulish agendas. I could give you other scenarios but more importantly, I want to pray for you.

> **If your soul is in a battle I want the Holy Spirit to reveal it to you.**
>
> *Lord, I pray that you will show _____ (your name) any battles of her soul. I bind all pride, stubbornness and deception that would cause her to not see the battle or to not want to lay it down. Give her revelation and understanding.*
> **If you have identified a battle, then pray the following prayer:**
>
> *Lord, I run up the white flag of defeat. I was not able to win the battle of _____ _____ _____ _____ _____ (describe it). I give the battle to You today. Lord heal my emotions and restore every area that was wounded in this battle. I release and forgive myself and all those who unintentionally became victims to my soulish need. (You may want to list the people.)*

As I said earlier your WHY may not be just the same as my WHY. But your WHY will hold the key to your freedom just like my WHY did for me. Will it be in relationship to your father? From my personal experience and my experience as a counselor, I can answer, "most of the time." Is it possible it could be from something else, yes. My oldest daughter was raped as a virgin at the age of 17. She has not only had to work out situations related to her father, but as God began to minister to her and bring healing into her life, He showed her how she continually ended up in relationships that were degrading – relationships that put her in positions to be forced to do things she did not want to do. She was still trying to *"win"* in the rape situation. Once again there was no win – just greater wounding. However, I can attest to the healing power of God that has set her free and has caused her desires to be sanctified. GOD IS SO GOOD!

SEXUAL IMPRINTING – GOD'S DESIGN

Before I close this chapter, it's important for me to share about sexual imprinting. It has a tremendous impact whenever there has been rape, molestation, sexual abuse, same sex contact, and pornography. And for many it can be the answer to your WHY. Let me explain sexual imprinting. God created us for covenant. He created us so that our desire would be for our covenant spouse. Our first sexual contact as husband and wife in the sanctity of the marriage bed is one designed to forever imprint that desire into our bodies and souls. That is why so many people never really get over what they call *"their first love."* In a righteous world, it is a wonderful component God built into man and woman which keeps them desiring each other throughout their relationship. However, in a fallen world, the enemy has taken what God meant for good and has used it for evil. When sexual imprinting occurs through the things I mentioned above, sexual perversion is set in motion in the souls and bodies of men and women.

My husband and I have ministered to a number of men who had their first sexual contact through masturbation and pornography, good Christian men, some of them leaders in the church who continually fight a desire for masturbation and pornography. I've worked with rape and abuse victims like my daughter who are drawn to degrading relationships. This is why rape to a virgin has a much more devastating and long lasting effect than to someone who is not. Please don't misunderstand, I am not minimizing the pain and suffering from anyone who has experienced rape or sexual abuse of any kind. It just does not carry the imprinting factor that the same experience to a virgin does. This is why we as adults must work at keeping our children in a sexually safe environment.

If you have been victim of wrong sexual imprinting, I don't want to leave you with the impression that there is no hope. Sexual imprinting is powerful but it is not more powerful than the One who created it in us. Our God is a God of restoration. Restoration means to put things back to their original condition. God wants to put you back to your original condition, one where your imprinting creates covenant and not bondage.

> **Pray with me.**
>
> *Heavenly Father, I have seen where the enemy has taken that which was a good thing and has used it for evil in my life. I forgive*
> _____
> *for*
> _____
> _____
> _____.
>
> *I ask you to forgive me of all sexual sin (be specific). I ask You now to make my body and soul a clean slate where covenant can be written on them by my mate. I break all soul ties with anyone else I have had sexual contact with (name them and include pornography if applicable). Thank you for healing me and setting me free.*

Make sure you include the person you first had sex with if it was not your mate. Even if it was consensual sex, forgive them for taking what did not belong to them and of robbing you and your mate of the imprinting God designed to seal the covenant of marriage. If you are married, I would encourage you to share with your spouse what God has done by erasing the slate and have a special honeymoon night. Pray together that covenant would be imprinted into your sexual desires.

This is often the reason why people have affairs. They may love their spouse but something within them is trying to recreate imprinting from the past. A good example would be a woman whose first sexual experience is with an older man. She then marries a wonderful young man but continually finds herself drawn to older men and eventually has an affair with her boss. A bad woman? No, just one who had sexual imprinting was bad. As our children get old enough to discuss sex with them, it's important to tell them WHY their virginity is so important to their marriage; how God created their bodies and souls to be stamped by their first sexual encounter. Our message that it is wrong, bad or sinful obviously hasn't been working. We need to portray a loving God who knows how he created us and asks us not to do certain things because He knows it is going to create problems for us.

If you are not married but are no longer a virgin, pray and ask the Lord to forgive you and restore your spiritual virginity. If you become engaged, make sure your fiancée prays and asks the Lord to cleanse and purify his sexuality before your wedding night. Before your first sexual encounter, pray together. Ask God to use what He designed for your good and to cause covenant to be written on your bodies and souls. As you pray these prayers, the exact words you use are not important; it's the heart of your prayer that counts with God.

I am here to tell you that all the counseling in the world cannot change things for you like the recreating power of God restoring what was stolen by the enemy. Even great success and money cannot change this cycle. Just look at all the movie stars and recording artists who continually go back to relationships that are destructive. We can see the patterns of women who could have almost any man in the world but choose one that is an alcoholic who will one day end up battering her. Time after time these women end up covered by the vomit of destructive relationships. Counseling may help a person cope. It may help you fight against the forces of the enemy. But only counseling that brings in the restorative power of God will set you totally free. If you believe, I know God will do it for you. He did it for me. He's done it for my daughter and many others I have ministered to and He will do it for you. That's what Jesus died for – to set the captives free. O daughter of Zion, won't you be loosed from your captivity?

Please read Isaiah Chapter 52 before continuing.

Chapter 2

Shake Yourself From The Dust

I am writing this chapter while babysitting my beautiful granddaughter, Jordan. To our family, she represents the hope of a future that has been cleansed of generational sin by the blood of Christ through salvation and the confession of the sins of our family line.

THE DUST OF GENERATIONAL SIN

Isaiah 61:4 explains to us that one of the ministries of Jesus is to help us rebuild the old ruins. It says, *"They shall raise up the former desolations, And they shall repair the ruined cities, The desolations of many generations."* If we study our generational histories, many times we discover that we are involved in sins that have been predominating in our families. Most of the time, you will find the same types of sin in the generational history of women who keep gravitating to relationships that are destructive. Sometimes the dust we must shake ourselves from is heavy and thick as a result of layers and layers of generational sin. At this point, we might be tempted to say, *"Well then there's just no hope."*

However, that is what the *Good News* is all about because with Christ there is hope. But we have to do our part. We must appropriate by faith what Christ did for us on the Cross and then we must *"do"* the Word. Generational sin opens the door to curses that were set in motion by God for those who did not practice the law. But once we accept Christ, we can set Galatians 3:13 into spiritual motion in our lives. It says, *"Christ has redeemed us from the curse of the law, having become a curse for us (for it is written, Cursed is everyone who hangs on a tree)."*

Just as every person is not saved simply because Jesus died on the cross for them, not everyone walks in the redemption that they could. Not everyone walks in their healing, even though we were healed by His stripes. And not everyone walks in their deliverance just because

Christ died to set the captives free. WHY? Because we must each individually appropriate our salvation, redemption, deliverance and healing by faith and DO the Word. That is why it is so important to be a DOER of the Word and not a hearer only (James 1:22-23). The same principle applies to redemption from generational sin. In the law, God continually reminded His people that there would be consequences for sin that would flow down to the generations, some to the third and fourth generations (Exodus 20:5), others even to ten generations (Deuteronomy 23:2). The scripture in Deuteronomy refers to the curse of illegitimacy. Those of illegitimate birth are not allowed to enter the assembly of the Lord even to the tenth generation of their descendants. I would call that a major curse!

I believe there are many people who just aren't able to participate in church because of this generational sin. I have experienced it first hand in the life of my oldest daughter. She was conceived before I was married and therefore was illegitimate in the eyes of God. Leanne was twelve years old when I was saved and started attending church. She would not enter into worship even when I would correct her for being so rude to God. I believe if we teach our children to have manners with man, we should also teach them to have manners with God. Once she got old enough, you could not get her inside of a church. I did not come to the revelation of generational sin until she was 24 years old. Sure I had repented of all my sin and knew that I was forgiven. But I hadn't really gone to the Throne of God about the sin of illegitimacy in particular as it related to myself and my family line. It was very evident by the number of my cousins who either became pregnant prior to marriage or caused a pregnancy before marriage.

I had to appropriate the redemptive blood of Christ for my daughter who had been cursed by my sin. Within a year, she rededicated her life to the Lord and for the first time was able to enter into congregational life and worship. Praise God! But it took more than me just singing *"I'm redeemed, I'm redeemed"* every Sunday morning. It took repentance and appropriation. More and more I have come to understand the scripture in Hosea 4:6 that says that we are destroyed for lack of knowledge and have forgotten the laws of our God. I want to personally thank Chester and Betsy Kylstra with *Proclaiming His Word Ministries* for helping to bring more understanding of the effects of generational sin through authoring *Restoring the Foundations*. Please see the Resource Section for more information on *Proclaiming His Word Ministries*.

Over and over in scripture, we see the answer for generational sin is confession. In Leviticus 26:39-42, it says, *"And those of you who are left shall waste away in their iniquity in your enemies' lands; also in their fathers' iniquities,* **which are with them**, *they shall waste away. but if they confess their iniquity and the iniquity of their fathers, with their unfaithfulness in which they were unfaithful to Me, and that they also have walked contrary to Me, and that I also have walked contrary to them and have brought them into the land of their enemies; if* *their uncircumcised hearts are humbled, and they accept their guilt - then I will remember My covenant with Jacob, and My covenant with Isaac and My covenant with Abraham I will remember; I will remember the land."* To do the Word, we must confess and repent for the iniquity of our forefathers. In John 20:23 after Jesus had breathed on the disciples and said to them, *"Receive the Holy Spirit,"* He then told them, *"If you forgive the sins of any they are forgiven them; if you retain the sins of any, they are retained."*

THE DUST OF VICTIMIZATION

Many women involved in destructive and abusive relationships come from family lines where women have been victimized for generations. They have a victim mentality. Once we are born again, we are new creatures in Christ, and it is sin to continue to walk in a victim mentality. The Word of God says that we are overcomers. However, it is not always easy to walk out of it, especially if it has been a way of life modeled for generations.

The flip side of the victim mentality is what I call the *"I won't stand for anything – I'm out of here"* mentality. At first glance, it doesn't look like the victim mentality because it comes across so strong and will not tolerate anything that even smells like wrong treatment. However, at its very base is still the belief that I am a victim and I must run from every situation where it looks like someone might mistreat or take advantage of me. This can happen in job situations, friendships, marriages, within ministries and in other relationships. The victim does not believe that they can overcome in a problem situation – they can only run from it.

True deliverance is when we believe that through the Power of God we can overcome in situations and we can be led by the Holy Spirit when to stay or when we must leave. Flight is not the automatic answer anymore. One side of the victim mentality makes a person stay and suffer and the flip-side makes them run at the first sight of anything that might be uncomfortable. We will examine the victim mentality further in the next chapter as we discuss thought processes that erect spiritual strongholds in our minds.

Some women have the weight of generational sexual sins and lust causing that extra pressure that makes them buckle to temptation. Remember, women, there is no answer to sexual sin except repentance. Marriage does not fix sexual sin – only repentance does. We would probably be amazed at the number of marriages that were the result of women who sinned sexually then tried to fix it through marriage. If I robbed a store, I could not fix it by working for the store for the rest of my life. In Christ, the only thing that works is repentance not my penance. Penance cannot be found in the New Testament. Restitution – yes! Penance – no!

Women often have generational fear related to provision. They would rather be with anybody instead of being alone and taking care of themselves. I can't tell you the heartache pastors go through when they see precious women of God so desperate to have a man in their life. Unless set free, they will end up in unequally yoked marriages just so they have someone taking care of them. I've seen Christian women who have just been released from marriage as a result of adultery by husbands with alcohol and drug problems go right back to a different man with the same problems with a man that is still having problems with alcohol or drugs.

I don't care if these men say they are Christians – ARE THEY LIVING A CHRISTIAN LIFE? And have they lived that lifestyle for a period of time or did they just happen to find Jesus when you came along? The Word tells us to test the spirit, yet women drawn to these type of relationships will jump at anyone who comes along. They will not allow time to try the fruit of these men's lives. Fear is sin in God's eyes and must be confessed. Do you trust God's Word that says He will provide for you or do you live in fear of being on your own? The sad thing that I see so often is that the women who end up gravitating to a relationship that is security related often are the ones providing the real financial support and stability to the family anyway.

You can shake off generational dust by asking God to forgive you and your forefathers for sins that can result in destructive relationships.(Sins of rebellion, being unteachable, fear, lust, insecurity, fear of rejection, fear of not being provided for, unbelief, victim thinking, unworthiness, pride, enabling, addictions, and occult involvement are a good place to begin, and then just ask the Holy Spirit to show you any others that may not be listed here.)

Lord, I confess the sins of my fathers and my own sin of

_____

_____

_____.

I break any agreement with these sins of

_____

_____

and loose my life from any demons assigned to the resulting curses. I apply the shed blood of Jesus Christ to these sins now and thank you for my redemption and for redeeming the generations to come. Amen

THE DUST OF UNFORGIVENESS

Another major area of dust (or past) we need to shake off is unforgiveness. This is very dangerous dust because we are required in Scripture to forgive as we have been forgiven. We are told in Matthew 18:21-35 through a parable that we will be turned over to the tormentors as a result of unforgiveness. These tormentors represent demonic spirits. Women who have not truly forgiven their fathers and other men in their lives open themselves up to ongoing relationships that bring torment. Their pathway to freedom is through forgiveness. Forgiveness does not mean what the person did was right or okay, it simply means that in the light of God's forgiveness for us, we are able to release that person into God's hands to be dealt with as He sees fit. The Word tells us that *"vengeance is the Lord's."* Forgiveness is our first step towards healing.

I can't tell you how many times I've heard people execute their own sentencing when they say, *"I'll never forgive him for what he did to me"* or something very similar. It may be difficult to forgive and it may take time. But you have to start someplace, if not, you create your own prison. Forgiveness is an act of obedience. It is not a feeling. Most people want to wait until they feel it in their heart. They may wait a lifetime. There is no place in God's Word that says when you feel forgiveness overflowing from your heart then forgive that person. It simply says, *"Forgive as you have been forgiven."*

I have found in my own life and through counseling hundreds of people that forgiveness is a process. It starts with confession, and then it must be confronted with action and finally worked into our hearts until our spirit and soul experience a total release. Anyone who has worked through to the depths of forgiveness knows that moment when you want to shout, *"I'm free – I'm really free, at last!"* Sometimes the process can be accomplished in moments and other times, in the case of deep wounding, I've seen it take years. As long as God knows we are pressing into forgiveness, His mercy and forgiveness is always available to us. When we quit the process prematurely, throw up our hands and say, *"I'll never really be able to forgive,"* that's when we get ourselves into spiritual trouble.

One of the tactics of the enemy to hinder the forgiveness process is to cause the very individuals we are trying to forgive to keep doing things that continually rewound. Another way is to cause similar situations to happen even if it is with different faces. The familiarity of it stirs up the old wounds and causes us to feel the pain again. That, in turn, makes us have to forgive all over again. The devil loves for us to stay in a place of unforgiveness because it gives him a spiritually legal right to torment us. No matter how many binding prayers we pray, how many warfare songs we sing and how much we rebuke him, God allows him to torment us. Now why would a loving God do that? Because He wants us to forgive so we can once again enter into His

Presence where we find freedom, joy and peace. When we finally come to a place where we are willing to do anything for relief, we will forgive. It is like an instant *Get Out of Jail Card*.

If you are living or have lived in a toxic, destructive relationship, shake yourself from the dust of unforgiveness. Allow the Holy Spirit to minister to you. Don't try to do this from your own mind or memory. Get quiet before the Lord and ask him what men in your life you need to forgive. Make sure to tell the Lord exactly why you're forgiving them. For example, I forgive my father for never spending time with me and causing me to feel like if he didn't love me, who else would. I forgive my brother for talking about girls without any respect and making me feel that all men would just use me and not really value me, etc.

> *Lord, I ask you to release a spirit of forgiveness and grace to the women reading this who really want to forgive the men in their lives who have hurt them, betrayed them, rejected them, and abandoned them. Help them, Lord, to release their pain to you. Holy Spirit, I ask you to bring to mind everyone they still have some measure of unforgiveness towards whether it's a man or woman so they may totally be set free from the prison of unforgiveness and bitterness.*

Once you have forgiven others, then it's time to forgive yourself. Also, even though we aren't in the spiritual position to be able to forgive God, sometimes we have to be honest with Him and repent for our anger, unforgiveness and bitterness towards Him. Always remember, it is the sins of our forefathers, our own personal sins, and the work of the devil that brings pain and suffering in our lives. God is not your problem. He is waiting for you with open arms to bind up your wounds and to protect you from your tormentors.

The key to getting from where you are to the loving arms of Jesus is forgiveness. The act the person did may have ruined a part of your life – your unforgiveness can ruin your entire life! Shake yourself from the dust of unforgiveness – it's just not worth holding!

Chapter 3

Loose Yourself From The Bonds

One of the saddest types of bondage I have seen over the years in the lives of Christian women works like a bungee cord. A bungee cord will give a good ways but still keeps you tied to whatever it is hooked to. It makes you think you're free but you're really not. These women begin a life in Christ with a real desire for things to be different. They develop prayer lives and attend church regularly. Then it happens, the one man comes along (usually sent by the enemy) and that bungee cord of bondage snaps them back. The hook was never fully removed and suddenly they are pulled out of the things of God. Soon they are doing things they said they would never do again.

It is so important that when our spiritual lives are going well that we take time with the Lord to allow Him to show us areas that need ministry. Usually when things are going well people don't ask for help. They often turn to counseling in times of crisis. From years of working in this arena, I can tell you the worst time to get true ministry is during a crisis because all you are concentrating on is on the pain you feel at the moment. If people would seek and *receive* good premarital counseling, we could drastically reduce the amount of marriage counseling that is necessary. If we would allow God to minister to us when all is well, we wouldn't have to live from crisis to crisis. In every form of natural medicine preventative measures are always the best. The same is true with spiritual medicine. If you have had relationships that weren't healthy, take time to ask God to show you the root problems. If you leave an ungodly, unhealthy root system in place, it will always regrow the fruit eventually. Loose yourself from the bonds.

I want to talk about four important bonds that can pull us back into destructive relationships. They are vows, judgments, ungodly beliefs and soul ties. I used a vow in the very first paragraph of this chapter. *"I will never get involved in a relationship like that again."* It becomes a judgment when we add things to the vow such as *"I will never have bad relationships like my mother always did"* or *"I'll never be like my sister who kept going back to that alcoholic husband of hers."* Vows and judgments often work hand and hand.

LOOSING THE BONDS OF VOWS

Let's look at vows first. Why are they so dangerous and why can a vow made as a child continue to affect our lives as an adult Christian? Vows are related to our wills. When we vow we usually say either out loud or in our hearts, "I **will**... or I **will** never ..." The one thing that God will not violate is the **will** of man. He created us with a free will. That is why it is so special to Him when we choose to live for Him and become like Him out of our own free will. However in our ignorance, this gift from God can create havoc in our life.

When we vow, we take that portion of our life out of God's hands. We declare that through our own strength, will, determination, intelligence, etc. we will get the job done. It takes us away from relying on God's grace and power and says, *"God, I'm going to be in charge of this area of my life and handle it in my own strength."*

"I'll never let anyone hurt me like that again."
"I'll never let anyone walk all over me again."
"I'll never get divorced again."
"I'll never really open up to anyone again."
"I'll never trust men again.

I could go on and on because I've heard so many of them. Usually the person is right back in the same situation that they declared would never happen again. People who say they will never let anyone hurt them again build up such emotional walls that they are constantly in a state of hurt, loneliness and rejection. We need to say, *"By God's grace and mercy, He will give me relationships that will bless me and not wound me"* or *"With God's help, I am going to have a happy marriage."* Those are positive faith statements that allow God into those areas of our lives. A vow closes God out and He allows us to see just how powerful we are without Him. (Not very powerful at all!) That is why we must be able to say as Jesus did, "Nevertheless, *not My will but Your will be done."*

> **Ask the Holy Spirit to show you any vows that you have made and then pray...**
>
> *Lord, please forgive me for having made the vow that*
> _____
> _____
> _____
> _____.
>
> *I break the power of those words over my life now, and I release that portion of my life back to Your authority, power and grace.*

LOOSING THE BONDS OF JUDGMENTS

Now let's look at how judgment affects us. The Word of God tells us in Matthew 7:1-2, *"Judge not, that you be not judged. For with what judgment you judge, you will be judged; and with the measure you use it will be measured **back to you.**"* I used to think that meant that if I judged critically, I would be judged critically. If I released grace and mercy, then I would receive grace and mercy. I still believe that, but I also believe that judgment will come back to us in the very form that it was sent out. If I judge someone else on how they parent, I'll end up having problems with my kids. If I judged my mother on how she raised me, I'll treat my children the same way. If I judge someone for gossiping, I'll find myself doing the very same thing. Over and over as I have counseled people, I have found this to be true.

Why else would someone who was abused as a child ever put their child through the same thing? It is because of the spiritual laws related to vows and judgments. They vow with judgment in their heart against their parents that they will never treat their kids like they were treated. And the next thing they know they are doing the same thing and sometimes worse. They have taken God out of the equation through their vow. And then their judgment releases the same judgment back into their lives. Matthew 7:1-2 *"Judge not, that you be not judged. For with what judgment you judge, you will be judged; and with the measure you use, it will be measured back to you."* Now **their** children are hurt and angry for how they are being treated and are having the same feelings about them that they had towards their parents.

Many of the women who continue to be involved in toxic relationships are ones that vowed something like this, *"I'll never allow a man to treat me the way my mother let my father treat her."* The Word of God says in Ephesians 6:2-3, "Honor *your father and mother,"* which is *the first commandment with promise: "that it may be well with you and you may live long on the earth."* When we dishonor our parents through judgment, it sets in motion the law of sowing and reaping, and we end up receiving the same judgment from our children. It's important to understand that this does not mean you are saying what your parents did was right. It simply means you are not going to play God and judge them.

As children, if we were not raised in godly homes, we didn't understand this. Many of us entered into judgment of our parents. Now, as adult Christians, we must repent for this sin. John and Paula Sanford who are pioneers in the areas of healing for the inner man believe that in every area where life is not going well for us, we can go back to our relationships with our parents and find areas where we dishonored our parents. I highly recommend their DVD on Bitter Root Judgments. Please see the recommended resources guide at the end of the book for more information on their ministry.

Let's stop once again and allow the Holy Spirit to minister. Ask Him to show you areas where you have judged your parents and how they treated one another or maybe where you judged other women who were in bad relationships.

Even though we are focusing on this area of unhealthy relationships, you may want to take the time and examine other areas in your life that have not been going well and ask the Lord to show you if there are any other judgments that you need to repent for.

Here's a simple prayer...

Lord, forgive me for judging _____ for how they _____ _____.

(If it was related to your parents also add, "forgive me for dishonoring my mother and/or father.") I now curse the harvest this judgment produced in my life and rebuke every demon from this cycle of sowing and reaping.

LOOSING THE BONDS OF UNGODLY BELIEFS

The third area that can cause us to be pulled back into bondage is through ungodly root thought patterns. The Kylstra's call them Ungodly Beliefs, the Sanford's call them Bitter Root Expectancies, and in secular counseling in rational emotive therapy they are called Irrational

Ideas. These are thoughts that have been programmed deep into our subconscious minds through years of experience and reinforcement. Even when we know what the Scriptures say, these reinforced thought patterns can try to tell us something else.

Let me give you an example. God's Word tells us that we are *"accepted in the beloved."* But if we were rejected by our parents, rejected by the kids at school and rejected by men in our lives, our Ungodly Belief System Printout would probably read, **"Something must be terribly wrong with me, I better keep my distance or I will get rejected again."** It causes our behavior to be different and strained. Because people are uncomfortable around us we end up experiencing more rejection. This brings more reinforcement as our subconscious minds say, *"See, I told you it was true, everyone will reject you."* It's why many people have such difficulty becoming a part of a church body and church life. They have such fear of rejection.

If this fear is deep enough, it can open up to a spirit of rejection. Then a person may need deliverance also. However, deliverance, without attacking the stronghold built in the person's mind through years of reinforced experience, usually proves to give temporary relief, if anything. The spirit simply returns to the safety of the stronghold and sets up residency once again. This is why 2 Corinthians 10:4-5 says, "For *the weapons of our warfare are not carnal but MIGHTY in God for pulling down strongholds, casting down arguments and every high thing that exalts itself against the knowledge of God, bringing every thought into captivity to the obedience of Christ."* If we are going to be victorious in spiritual warfare against the enemy, we must dismantle the strongholds within our thought lives. We must realize that our experiences produce fact but only those beliefs which align themselves with God's Word are TRUTH. We have to decide are we going to base our lives and responses on facts or truth.

When we believe things that are not in accordance with the Word of God, we are coming into agreement with the enemy and giving him a right to be involved in those areas of our lives. In Exodus, God told the Israelites not to make any covenants with their enemies; if they did, they would have to serve them. When we are still in covenant with the enemy in our minds, we end up in bondage in that area of our lives. To loose the bonds, we must give up our ungodly beliefs and renew our mind to what the Word of God says.

Romans:12:2 "And *do not be conformed to this world, but be transformed by the renewing of your **mind**, that you may prove what is that good and acceptable and perfect will of God."* This scripture tells us that becoming like Christ is a process and does not happen simply through our born again experience. Ephesians 4:23-24 *"and that you put off, concerning your former conduct, the old man which grows corrupt according to the deceitful lusts, and be renewed in the **spirit of your mind**, and that you put on the new man which was created according to God, in true righteousness and holiness."* These scriptures tell us that our thought life is the key to our Christian walk.

Here are a few examples of Ungodly Beliefs that I have seen in operation which keep women going back to the vomit of bad relationships:

- *"I'm really not that _____(pretty, smart, thin, etc.) so I better not be too picky."*
- THE CLASSIC: *"He'll change once he has a good woman in his life."*
- *"I can't make it alone – I have to have a man in my life, so even a bad man is better than no man at all."*
- *"If I don't just believe him when he says he's going to change and want to see evidence before proceeding, it means I don't have faith."*
- *"Even though he's always had trouble with authority in his family, on the job, even in church, he will receive from me; I can change him."*
- *"It's really my fault he _____ (drinks, loses his temper, hits me, does drugs, lusts after other women, etc.). When I _____ (lose weight, act nicer, become more understanding, learn to be more loving, become a better housekeeper, etc.), he will change."*
- *"You can't really expect to have communication and relationship with a man; that's just the way they are."*
- *"Even though he has had trouble in all of his other relationships, it's going to be different with me."*
- *"Having a man desire me means I have self-worth."*
- *"All men are the same, they ...."*

All of the above and many more ungodly beliefs are at the root of a tree that will continue to produce bad fruit in relationships. Even if it looks like it has been chopped down, if the root system is not dealt with, it will grow back. It's one of the reasons why we see Christian women ending up back in bad relationships even after years of serving the Lord.

In order to get to these thought processes that produce toxic results in our lives, we must seek the Lord and be willing to get painfully honest. We also need to be willing to hear the truth of why we do what we do. We have to start recognizing and laying down every defense mechanism of denial, justification, rationalization and self-deception. We must desire truth in the inward parts.

Allow the Lord to show you how these ungodly beliefs got planted in your life and forgive the people who helped reinforce them. Next work at creating new beliefs that align themselves with the Word of God. For example, let's take the first few of the previous ungodly beliefs and create new godly beliefs:

- *"Because I am the apple of God's eye, I can trust that as I am patient to wait for God's best, He will provide a man fit for the daughter of a King."*
- *"The only transforming power in a man's life is the power of God."*
- *"Because the Lord is my provider, I can trust Him to meet all of my needs."*
- *"God says to know people by their fruit/actions not by what they say."*
- *"Wives are to be submitted to their husbands for their safety and protection. Their husbands must be submitted to God by submitting to the Word and spiritual and natural authority."*

Can you see the major differences in fruit that these belief systems would produce? Once you get honest with God and yourself and identify your ungodly beliefs, repent for believing the lies, forgive the people who helped you believe that way and then create new godly beliefs. Then comes the hard part that takes discipline, your mind must now be renewed. This takes meditating on the truth for a period of time. I recommend reading your new godly beliefs two to three times a day for a minimum of 40 days depending on the depth of the ingrained ungodly beliefs.

The reason I say a minimum of 40 days is because of an attribute of Satan that is revealed in the Word. Satan is called Beelzebub. Beelzebub means *"Lord of the Flies."* This name was given to him so we could have insight into his operations. We can study flies to help understand how Satan works. Flies have a 40 day life cycle. When we resist the enemy for 40 days, he is defeated without the ability to reproduce. That's why there were so many 40 day fasts in the Bible.

You may want to record your list on and listen to them while you drive. Post them on a bathroom mirror. Keep a copy in your car, etc. You will find by changing your beliefs new expectations will ignite and cause faith to arise and activate within you. As your faith changes, your behavior changes and so will the behavior of people around you.

> *Lord, forgive me for believing (state the ungodly belief)*
> _____
> _____
> _____.
>
> *I forgive (name the people)_____*
> *for (what did they do that reinforced this ungodly belief?)*
> _____
> _____
> _____
> _____ *which caused me to continue believing that way.*
>
> *I renounce this ungodly belief and any area of agreement with the enemy and break its power over my life now. Holy Spirit, I ask you to convict me of any thoughts, habits, or actions related to this ungodly belief. From now on, I choose to believe (state the godly belief).*

As you begin this process related to relationships, you will find the Holy Spirit will begin to illuminate other areas of stinking thinking to you. He has a desire to lead us into all truth and is just waiting for us to be willing to allow Him to do a deep work in us. He has been sent by the Father to help prepare a bride without spot or wrinkle for Jesus. He delights in ministering to us; all we have to do is make ourselves available and willing. Our conscious minds may tell us we believe one thing, but there might be something else at work. The fruit of our lives tells us what the root system is really like. To get free from toxic relationships, we must get free from toxic thought processes.

LOOSING THE BONDS OF UNGODLY SOUL TIES

The last bond we are going to look at in this chapter is soul ties. These are ties that bind us to people as a result of sexual activity, long term relationships, and even trauma experienced with another person can create a soul tie. This is why people involved in certain crime situations can sometimes open their souls and become tied to the very one committing the crime. Even though one part of a person who has been molested or abused as a child hated the perpetrator and what they did, another part of them may still have an emotional or soul tie to the individual.

Jesus confronted soul ties when He told his disciples that they must leave mother, father, brother, lands, etc. in order to follow Him. A soul tie is any relationship that has more power over your life than the Lord. They are idolatrous in the sense that our souls put the individual or thing above God. We can have ungodly soul ties with parents, children, friends, sports, a church or ministry, money, animals, past relationships, and just about anything else. In our family and close relationships, our soul can and should be very much involved in the relationship. It's only when it takes preeminence over our relationship with the Lord that problems develop. For example, God may be telling you to go on a ministry trip; four hours before you are to leave, your six year old develops a tummy ache. Do you automatically stay home? If you have ungodly soul ties, you would. If you don't, you would pray and ask the Lord what to do. If the Lord said go, then you would go trusting that the child would be fine. As long as the enemy knows you have soul ties with certain individuals, he will always stir up situations in their lives to control you through them.

Soul ties pull us back to what is familiar. I have seen women loosed from marriage, because their husbands committed adultery and abandoned them, go right back into relationships with men that were totally similar. Why? Because the soul ties hadn't been completely broken with the first man they were drawn to what was familiar. The soul identification opened up the door for another bad relationship even though it was not what the Lord had for her. If soul ties haven't been broken with an abusive father, a woman may continue to seek out relationships with abusive men. It's so sad because the very thing her soul needs for healing is a man who will love and cherish her, yet it seeks out the familiar.

There are two responses when dealing with soul ties. The first is to identify those we have soul ties with, pray a prayer of repentance and break their power off of our life. The second and most important is to build our spirit man. When our spirit man is strong enough, it will no longer tolerate the pull of soulish relationships. The Word of God tells us that when we sow to the flesh, we reap flesh and if we sow to the spirit we reap spirit. Our spirit man is built up by studying the Word of God and through prayer. Paul says in 1 Corinthians 14: 4 that *"he who speaks in a tongue edifies himself."* *Edify* means to build up or strengthen. And in Ephesians 6, the spiritual warfare chapter, Paul also exhorts us to pray always in the Spirit. Many people want to pray a simple prayer which is the beginning of breaking soul ties but for complete victory our spirit man must become strong. The first wins the initial battle; the second wins the war! Both are important.

> **Ask the Lord to show you individuals who you may still have soul ties with and then let's pray...**
>
> *Lord, I repent for allowing my life to be controlled by ungodly soul ties, and I ask you to forgive me. I also ask you to forgive me for any sexual and physical activities (be specific) that opened the door to ungodly soul ties. I break the power of ungodly soul ties with _____ (name the individuals) over my life now. Please set me free so that I can be led by your Spirit and governed by your Word.*

That's the beginning; now it's important to build your spirit man through time spent reading and studying the Word of God, through prayer and worship. As we went over these four areas of vows, judgments, ungodly beliefs and soul ties, I hope you noticed that the answers continue to be the same over and over again. Repentance and forgiveness – repentance and forgiveness – repentance and forgiveness. Those two elements working together in the heart of a believer release the power of God necessary for freedom. Never underestimate their importance. Sometimes we want to look for more complicated answers or easier answers. Repentance and forgiveness are pretty simple answers but not always easy. It takes the grace of God working in our lives. Loose yourself from the bonds – repent and forgive.

Chapter 4

You Have Sold Yourself For Nothing

Many women end up in toxic, destructive relationships because their self-worth is so low. They don't really believe they deserve or can have anything any better. **They sell themselves for nothing because they don't know their value.** The first man to give them a little bit of interest or attention can hook them easily. Instead of believing for God's best in their lives, they end up with the enemy's worst. They allow themselves to be used sexually because of feeling it is the only thing they have to offer.

Instead of patiently trusting God's timing to bring them the best, they settle. These women become masters of excuses, denial, rationalization and justification: *"He would have a good job, it's just no one understands him, he's so much smarter than the people he's worked for... He would be in church; he's just never had a pastor who really cared about him... The reason he has no relationship with his children is because his ex-wife gives him such a hard time... The reason he's pressuring me sexually is because he just wants me so bad and it's like we are already married in the spirit."* And it goes on and on. Anything but the truth – that he has a rebellion problem and has never submitted to anyone's authority. He is not willing to submit to church authority because he's independent and self-sufficient. He's selfish and a poor father and it was just easier for him to walk away from his children. He's full of lust and is not only willing to sin in his own life, but also has so little regard and respect for you that he will pressure you into sin and the shame that goes with it. There are no right reasons for doing the wrong things!

Out of the fear of providing for yourself, you can open up to a spirit of harlotry. You may be saying wait a minute, *"I have never prostituted myself."* No, you may have not sold yourself directly but you may have indirectly... *"I am going to marry him because he has a good job, a nice house and car. I'll be safe, secure and provided for."* You have just sold yourself. *"The only reason I am staying is because I can't take care of myself."* You just sold yourself. *"The more sexual I am with him the more he gives me gifts and treats me nice."* You just sold yourself. *"I can't stand living at home any longer, I'm just going to get married."* You just sold yourself.

There are many ways you can open yourself up to the spirit of harlotry and prostitution. There are probably more prostitutes living in suburban homes than walking the streets of our cities. They are women who have sold themselves because of their fear, their greed or their lack of self-worth. And deep down in their spirits, their husbands know it, too. Allow the Holy Spirit to examine your hearts and motives. If you feel this could be a problem, just pray this prayer with me.

> *Lord, I repent for wrong motives in relationships with men, even my own husband (if married). I command every spirit of fear, greed, prostitution and harlotry to leave me now in the Name of Jesus Christ. I choose to trust You as my provider. You are my source and my heart will trust in You.*

SAFETY IN A MULTITUDE OF COUNSEL

Some women want to have a man in their life so badly that they will do anything to avoid seeing the man's true condition. They will close their eyes to what they see and their ears to even their close friends and family as they try to point out potential problem. Let me give you a CLUE: When your pastors, your close friends, your family and your own prayer partner are saying, "Stay *away from this guy, he's not the one."* The answer is not to remove yourself from fellowship with them. They are not the enemy trying to keep you from the love of your life. They are seeing something you're not because you are being blinded and deceived. LISTEN TO THEM! If they are all wrong, God is big enough to change their hearts. But what if they are right, what if you end up in another relationship from hell? What if all of his charm is demonic and manipulative? What if his undying love for you is just lust? What if he has a deep down hatred for women and he first has to capture your love so then he can hurt you? What if his spirituality is just a ploy to seduce you? I have seen all of the above scenarios and more. I have seen intercessors, women in ministry, women who have been Christians for years all fall into the trap even when people have tried to stop them. It's not just the baby Christians who become ensnared.

I have repeatedly counseled women, *"If it's really God and he really loves you, you don't have to be in such a hurry. Take time to know him. If he says he's going to change areas in his life wait until you see the changes in evidence over a period of time."* But if your self-worth is low, you will be too afraid that if you don't hurry into it, this one will get away. And then there might not be anything better out there for you. You don't want to hear counsel that advises you to slow down and you will reject it and the people sharing it.

Where does self-worth come from anyway? In our Christian walk, it is supposed to come from believing what God has said about us in His Word. It comes from accepting that Jesus Christ loved us so much that we were worth dying for. However, if we don't take the time to renew our minds to what God says about us, we will keep looking at ourselves through the eyes of our past. Many of us still have on the eyeglasses of our childhood which color how we see ourselves and others.

Our natural self-worth comes from the input we receive as children, especially from our parents and close family members. If they happened to be critical and unable to give praise and encouragement, our self-worth can be affected. If we grew up in families that were poor, our self-worth suffers. Other children had more... nicer clothes, better toys, they lived in nicer homes, and something in us said that we must be worth less. The mind of a child is not able to compute that it was the generational and/or territorial curses of poverty, sin in their family's lives, rebellion against God and everything else that can cause poverty that affected their lives. The child does not realize it was not them – they were not less than anyone else just because they had less.

Other people can come from prosperous families, but if they were constantly criticized about how they look and what they did, their self-worth suffers. Name calling is painful and word curses are powerful. The book of James Chapter 3 tells us that we can bless men or curse them with our tongues. Curses are empowered demonically; blessings are empowered by God and His angelic forces. Blessings release the work of the Holy Spirit in our life to bring about what God desires for us. Our words are powerful. The Word tells us that the power of life and death is in the tongue. We were created in the image of God, and He created the entire earth and its inhabitants with the spoken word.

The self-worth of a child can be damaged by words spoken over them by family members, friends, schoolmates, teachers, etc. As I counsel and minister to people, it is amazing to see the effect words spoken in the past still have over them. Beautiful, thin women still feel ugly and fat because of being teased as children. Intelligent women who were constantly told they were stupid or what they did was stupid by their mother or father are left totally insecure and afraid to try anything because they don't think they are smart enough. Women, who have been told as children that no one would ever want them or they are so bad no one will love them, will end up settling for less, even mistreatment in relationships.

If we value something, we take care of it. When children are raised in homes where there was neglect or abuse, their self-worth suffers. It doesn't matter if it was a household that was poor or wealthy. Neglect and lack of attention and affection affect self-worth. It says, *"You are not important or valuable enough for my time or my care."* I have ministered to wealthy people who were sent off to boarding schools or were cared for by servants and they suffered from low self-worth, yet, they were given everything money could buy. They didn't feel that they were important enough to be cared for by their parents. Parents are essential in providing self-worth.

But what happens if we didn't receive what we needed from our natural families? They didn't give us the necessary elements to provide a sense of self-worth and confidence. Does God leave us undone? No! His Word declares that even when our mother and father forsake us then He will take care of us. (Psalm 27:10) When we receive the love of the Lord and the revelation that He created us for a purpose and a destiny, we begin to recognize our value. We must then renew our minds to what God says about us in His Word.

DAUGHTERS OF A KING

When we really get the revelation that we are Daughters of a King, we will start examining our relationships in that light. Would the King choose this man as suitable for his daughter? I have found that women who will accept less – get less. Even if you are in a relationship, you can begin to set healthy boundaries of what type of treatment you will or will not accept. If you are in a relationship, use this as a rule of thumb: would this type of treatment be suitable for a Daughter of a King? If not, why are you accepting it?

If you are not in a relationship, examine the next man in your life through the eyes of this revelation. Is this individual suitable for the Daughter of a King? Does he treat you with respect … does he have the ability to provide for you … does he have the revelation that you are the Daughter of a King? Now you have to use balance in this revelation because our Heavenly King has different values and priorities than the kings of this world. Earthly kings may provide their daughters with palaces and riches but our Heavenly King provides His Daughters with the Kingdom of God which is righteousness, peace and joy in the Holy Ghost. You must have an understanding of your Heavenly Father's value system in order to know what you should expect as an inheritance, and the only way you can do that is to study His Word for yourself.

Let's pray ...

*Heavenly Father, I repent for allowing myself to be mistreated and not cared for properly. I ask you to forgive me for my low self-worth and taking on the value that other people or my past experiences have ascribed to me. I forgive all of the individuals_____
who have devalued me through their words and actions (describe). Please help me to receive the revelation that I truly am a Daughter of a King and heal my sense of self-worth.*

Chapter 5

Touch No Unclean Thing

Once we have dedicated our lives to the Lord, it is so important that we remember the title of this chapter, *"Touch no unclean thing."* I am going to be totally open in this section and share what I have found to be true over and over again. The greatest hook that the enemy often has in women to pull them back into destructive relationships that bring bondage in their lives is lust. Their own sexual desires hold the key to their captivity.

Lust must be fought on two fronts: it comes from without as a demonic spirit and it comes from within our carnal nature. It was the lust of the eyes, the lust of the flesh and the pride of life that caused the first man and woman to fall into sin and that sin nature continues to war within us. The demonic spirit must be fought through warfare, through deliverance – casting out the demonic spirit, and by keeping the spiritual doors closed. The lust within our carnal nature must be crucified but it cannot be done just through our own will power. We have already proven that our wills are no match – we eat too much, indulge ourselves, procrastinate and fall into sexual sin. It is only when the spirit man is empowered with the Holy Spirit that we have a power within us greater than our own carnal nature and the lust of our flesh.

DEMONS MUST HAVE DOORS

All demonic activity has to come through an open door in the spirit realm. Demons must have a place of access. Many times the doors to the demon of lust were opened even as children. Sometimes it can come through childhood sexual play and exploration, masturbation at a young age, exposure to pornography, molestation, abuse, or premature sexual experiences in the teen age years. We already have discussed sexual imprinting and how to wipe the sexual slate clean. If you know you have had experiences that could have opened up the door to a spirit of lust, just command the spirit to leave in the Name of Jesus or ask someone to pray with you. His Word tells us that as believers we can cast out demons in His Name. These are very obvious doors, but there are some doors not so clearly marked where the enemy of lust has access.

The less obvious doors are those of romance novels, soap operas, R-rated movies, and music. Songs are very powerful and can take us back to places and times when we were involved in relationships that involved lust. Just listening to those songs can open the door once again. Many romance novels are very descriptive in relating experiences between men and women. Some are really soft-porn in a romantic wrapping. Soap operas have gotten progressively worse and feature men and women involved in sexual relationships outside the sanctity of marriage. By allowing these types of things in your home and into you through the eye gate and ear gate, you give access to the demon of lust. 2 Corinthians 7:1 says, *"Therefore, having these promises, beloved, let us cleanse ourselves from all filthiness of the flesh and spirit, perfecting holiness in the fear of God."*

WAKE UP!

In order to avoid falling into bondage again, a woman must cleanse herself from all unrighteousness in the sexual area. Many women who are alone also allow the spirit of lust to remain through masturbation. It keeps their sexual desires stirred and encourages fantasy at a time when God may want to put those desires to sleep. With your sexual passions awakened and your thoughts given way to fantasy, it can leave you vulnerable to the first man that gives you any attention whatsoever. He is alive and breathing and that's good enough for you! WAKE UP – TOUCH NO UNCLEAN THING! When the first thing you feel is the chemistry and physical attraction – WAKE UP – that's not love, it's lust. In Chapter 8: 4 the Song of Solomon tells us not to stir up desire or awaken love before its time.

Many times because there is no 11th commandment that clearly says, "Thou *shalt not masturbate,"* people are confused about the issue. I have even ministered to people who have been on the mission field that have been taught that this is the way to keep from falling into sexual sin. I'm here to tell you, you can't fight lust with lust. You can only fight it through holiness and denying your flesh.

I want to take the time here to share from a great deal of personal experience counseling in this area what we have found related to masturbation. First of all, it is addicting; many people are actually fighting an addiction in this area not just a spirit of lust. Once it becomes an addiction, it has double force and power in our lives. At that time, it also becomes a way to relieve stress and is no longer just a sexual experience. You then need the escape and physical release that it gives. Even though, from my experience, men tend to fall in to this trap more often than women and may masturbate daily or several times a day as their addiction gets worse, women still deal with this problem, also.

THE GREAT LIE

The great lie about masturbation is that once I am married, I will quit. Over and over again, experience proves that this is a fallacy. Instead of quitting, it is done deceptively and brings shame to the spouse who is hiding it. Also, masturbation is usually accompanied by fantasy and pornography which adds to the shame and increases the sin. I have actually counseled women who very early in their marriages, even on their honeymoons, have discovered their husbands masturbating. Tt was devastating to them. In marriages where there is masturbation, you find that because of their ability to satisfy themselves sexually, there is not the same need for each other. This allows strife and distance in the relationship to continue long past the time to make up. Couples who need each other sexually seek reconciliation in a timely manner.

Once masturbation has become an addiction, it must be attacked as an addiction. First, it must be recognized. If you have been masturbating from childhood, it will definitely be an addiction. The next step is to identify triggers. When does the desire occur? What causes you to run to that behavior? You must remove the triggers from your life. And then you must confess that without Christ you are powerless to stop it. You have to face your addiction on a *"one-day-at-a-time basis."* It's also important to find an accountability partner. This is probably the hardest with sexual addictions because people have more shame in this area. Our society has made it okay to get help for other addictions but sexual addictions still carry a stigma. However, part of getting out of this addiction is to become accountable. Pray to God to send you an accountability partner with whom you can be open and honest. Make sure when you are dealing with this type of addiction that it is someone of the same sex!

Two questions I always ask people who are dealing with whether masturbation is right or wrong are, *"Could you get up in the front of the church and say you had sex with your husband last night?"* (usually the answer is, *"yes"*) The second question is, *"Could you get up in front of the church and say that you masturbated last night?"* (the answer is always *"no"*) The fact that we will go to such lengths to hide the behavior and would not want to expose it should tell us that this is sin. Our God-given conscience is speaking to us. We do not need an eleventh commandment to know what is right and wrong.

I can't exhort you strongly enough that one of the greatest keys of not going back to the vomit of destructive relationships is to take the key of lust out of the devil's hand. It may not be an easy battle but it is one worth the fight. Without the lust, you will not be prey to self-deception. Lust will cause you to overlook the reality of who he really is because of your desire to have your physical needs met.

I have seen intercessors, ministers, worshippers, women who have walked with God for years fall prey to a relationship because the area of lust was not fully dealt with in their life. I exhort you to be open and honest with God and yourself; don't try to put a flower and a bow and romanticize your lust. I have seen the devastation of women who thought they were dedicated to the Lord but because of this unsanctified area (that they were too *"spiritual"* to deal with) they end up unequally yoked. Then they live with the frustration of trying to get an unspiritual man to be spiritual. One of the determining factors in this area is how much physical involvement there has been before marriage. In everyone that I have ever dealt with related to destructive relationships, there has been premarital sex. Now sometimes they try to fool themselves and God by having all kinds of physical contact but not actual intercourse. Then try to tell themselves they have not had sex before marriage. That is self-deception and a lie.

I challenge you ladies, be holy as God is holy! Save yourself for marriage! Find out if it is lust that is holding the relationship together or love birthed out of the direction and leading of the Holy Spirit. If this chapter has spoken to you, I have included a prayer for deliverance. The Word of God tells us in Matthew 12:28 that when we cast out demons, the Kingdom of God has come upon us. If you don't have as much of the Kingdom righteousness, peace and joy as you would like, it just might mean a demon is robbing it from you. My motto is *"when in doubt – cast it out."* What can it hurt to command a demon that's not there to go? But what can it hurt to leave a demon that is there because we do not cast it out?

> *In the Name of Jesus, I renounce all affiliation and agreement with the demons of lust, deception, perversion, pornography, fantasy, masturbation, addiction, uncleanness and defilement (Add any others that the Lord shows you and just list what you feel is applicable to your personal situation.) I command the spirit of _____ to leave me now. Get out of my mind, my memory, my emotions and my body.*

You can do this yourself or you may want someone else who you trust and know is under authority (so they have authority), to lay hands on you and together command the demons to go. After the deliverance, ask the Lord for a fresh infilling of His Holy Spirit and make sure you spend time in prayer and in the Word. You don't want your house swept clean and left empty; it needs to be swept clean and filled with the Glory of God.

> **Now it's time to deal with our flesh and that takes repentance first:**
>
> *Lord, I repent of all my past sexual sins (you may want to be more specific here). Lord, I confess my inability to keep myself pure, and I ask you, Holy Spirit, to strengthen me in this area. Convict me of any thought or deed that will lead me into sin again. Lord, send me an accountability partner, someone to disciple me in this area, pray for me and watch over my soul. Give me the grace each day to deny myself and help me to recognize and discern lust as lust. Keep me from deception, Lord. I plead the blood of Jesus over myself and my relationships, and I ask You to keep them righteous and holy.*

I don't know how else to say it, but it's just not worth it. The price paid for a few moments of being hugged, feeling physically attractive or having sexual satisfaction is just not worth living in a relationship where we are devalued, demoralized and eventually destroyed. I have often said that I would like to have a room with a lock and key where I can lock women up until the insanity passes. Once they come to their senses, we can let them out. They say, *"love is blind,"* but I don't believe that. The true saying should be, *"lust is blind."*

Chapter 6

Put On Your Beautiful Garments

Now we get to the good stuff. In Jeremiah, we see the process and priority of prophetic ministry in Chapter 1:10. First there is a rooting out, a pulling down, a destroying and a throwing down. Then there is a building and planting. We have been throwing down the plan of the enemy, rooting up our ungodly beliefs and destroying generational strongholds. Now it's time to *"put on our beautiful garments."* The garments of salvation must be put on, and we have a responsibility in that process.

> *I will greatly rejoice in the Lord,*
> *My soul shall be joyful in my God;*
> *For He has clothed me with the garments of salvation,*
> *He has covered me with the robe of righteousness,*
> *As a bridegroom decks himself with ornaments,*
> *And as a bride adorns herself with her jewels,*
> *For as the earth brings forth its bud,*
> *As the garden causes the things that are sown in it to spring forth,*
> *So the Lord God will cause righteousness and praise*
> *to spring forth before all the nations.*
> **Isaiah 61:10-11**

The Lord has provided the robes of righteousness and through the blood of Christ our filthy rags of sin and defilement have been washed and transformed into the clean white linen of the Bride of Christ. However, we must, by faith, put on our new garments and keep them on. Ephesians 4:21-23 tells us that we must put on the new man by being renewed in the spirit of our mind. The Word also says in 2 Corinthians 5:17, that we are new creatures and old things have passed away, all things are new. We must receive that by faith. I see a lot of new creatures going back to old relationships. All that proves is that they never fully received their salvation. The Word of God tells us to walk out our salvation with fear and trembling. It is something we must take very seriously.

THE HEART OF A DOG OR THE HEART OF A DAUGHTER?

I remember crying out to the Lord about women returning to the vomit of destructive relationships and He reminded me of the Scripture that says a *"dog returns to its own vomit"*. He then said, *"Kathy, the only answer is that they have a heart change; they still have the heart of a dog."* The Lord so wants to change our hearts, even our own hearts towards ourselves. Someone may be abusing you, but guess what, you are allowing yourself to be abused. The Word of God tells us to love our neighbors as ourselves. Our problem is we don't love ourselves enough to even expect to be treated with respect.

As I shared previously, I have been there. You can't tell me, *"you don't know what it's like"*, because I do. I also know that **no one changed but me**. I became a new creature and began to believe what the Word of God said about me. Something changed deep down in the inside of me that said I didn't deserve to be treated like this anymore. Many of us are in abusive relationships as a form of self-punishment and we are not even aware of it. Once we truly have the revelation that our sins have been forgiven, our subconscious minds can then accept the fact that we no longer deserve the punishment!

We must take off our sin identity as we put on the new man and the garments of our salvation. As I shared earlier, our minds must be renewed, and we need to replace our ungodly beliefs with new godly beliefs, especially the ungodly beliefs about ourselves. I call it the perversion plan of the enemy. Satan has always wanted to be like God - but he's not! One of God's chief attributes is that He is a creator. Satan is not. His only form of creation is perversion. He perverts us and then says, "look at my creation." God has a destiny for us and Satan has a plan of perversion and destruction. We need to identify that plan in order to expose the enemy in our life. What has Satan tried to create in you? *fear, anger, depression, lust, failure, stress, poverty, mistrust, abuse, etc.*

I think you get the point. Pray and ask the Lord to give you a list of the specific things that Satan has tried to create in you that are negative and destructive. Then renounce each item in the Name of Jesus. Then create a list of what the Lord says about you related to each item on the list: *full of faith, peaceful, joyful, pure, victorious, resting in the Lord, prosperous, trusting, cared for, etc*.

The next step is to take what God says about us and put it into a paragraph form and meditate on it a couple of times a day. This needs to continue until we actually begin to believe it. It is who we are in Christ. It is new seed being sown into the gardens of our heart, and it will surely produce a harvest.

> **For example:**
> I am a ***peaceful, joyful*** woman of God who is ***full of faith***. I am ***pure*** and live ***victoriously***. As I ***rest in the Lord***, I know I am ***cared for*** and ***prosperous***. I ***trust*** the Lord and know that I am a blessed daughter of the King of Kings. *(See the poem at the end of the book.)*

THE GARMENT OF MINISTRY

As we put on our new beautiful garments, we have to add the garment of ministry. It begins by first ministering unto the Lord through worship and prayer. Our new garments must be garments of praise, not those of heaviness. To put on the garments of praise, we must close the door to the past through forgiveness, repentance and healing. The past will keep you clothed in heaviness. Seeing your future and destiny in Christ will cause you to put on the garment of praise. Jeremiah 29:11 says, *"I know the thoughts that I think toward you, says the Lord, thoughts of peace and not of evil, to give you a future and a hope."* The Apostle Paul tells us in Philippian's 3:13-14, *"Brethren, I do not count myself to have apprehended; but one thing I do, forgetting those things which are behind and reaching forward to those things which are ahead, I press toward the goal for the prize of the upward call of God in Christ Jesus."*

Paul was a sinner, a murderer, but in Christ He knew He had been forgiven. Paul was able to take his eyes off of his past and walk in the glorious hope of his future.

As we minister unto the Lord first, He will then begin to uncover our giftings and anointings. We can then begin to minister to others. We begin to have compassion on others because we are not so caught up in our own pain. The love of the Lord begins to shine through us and because of our beautiful garments we begin to draw others to Christ. Just like in the natural, when we see someone in a beautiful dress, we want one too. The Lord wants us clothed in our beautiful garments of salvation for others to admire and decide they want robes of righteousness, also.

This can also be a dangerous time because we become even more attractive as our countenance is changed and actually unintentionally draw more attention from men. We must handle this in a righteous manner and know that they are being drawn to the Christ within. It is not a time to let our mercy so run away with us so that we end up in a relationship trying to *"minister"* to someone who we think is in need of rescuing. I have seen too many women end up with a recovering alcoholic, drug addict or someone right out of prison who did not wait long enough to make sure the recovery or transition time was completed. They can even short circuit the recovery process of the individual as they get involved in a personal relationship with them. They have a vision for what *"could be in God"*, but won't wait long enough to make sure that it *"will be in God"*. The results can be disastrous.

I was set free supernaturally from alcohol addiction and know that we can be delivered quickly, but I wouldn't have recommended anyone marrying me the next day, the next week, the next month or even the next year. I needed to walk out my recovery first. I am not saying that this type of relationship should never happen. Some of God's greatest ministers are ex-alcoholics, ex drug addicts and ex-convicts. I just want to emphasize knowing the timing of God and to be careful that our garments of ministry are not mistaken for garments of enabling and co-dependency.

It's your choice. Will you accept the beautiful garments of salvation or will you continue to hang on to the garments of condemnation, victimization, and self-rejection? The Lord has prepared the garments for you. As you accept Jesus as your personal Savior, He outstretches His hand with His own robe of righteousness, a beautiful garment... just for you. However, He won't force it on us. We must take it from His hand and begin to wear it. Sometimes it feels uncomfortable in the beginning. It is something unfamiliar. But the longer we continue to wear it, the more comfortable we become in our new garments. We as women always love a new outfit. Won't you try this one on today?

> *Dear Jesus, I thank you for Your shed blood that purchased my own personal robe of righteousness. I receive it today and ask you to give me the grace to wear it daily. Holy Spirit, please convict me if I try to take it off in my thought life, in my confession or in my emotions. Help me to walk in who I really am in Christ. Let your beauty shine through me.*

Chapter 7

Behold, It Is I

We have to know the one who loves us. Once we do, we don't have to run into the arms of men to have our needs met. We can be complete in Jesus Christ. He loves us. He died for us. He will provide for us. He guides us. And He sent His Comforter, the Holy Spirit, to walk with us on a daily basis. Once we become complete in Him, we can then have a healthy positive relationship – a relationship not based out of our need but a relationship based on what we have to give.

In marriage counseling, the major issues are unmet needs: the need for more conversation, more physical affection, more money, more time, more attention... *"I have needs that aren't being met."* The real root of most of these problems are individuals, both men and women who do not know how to have their needs met by the Lord. They place a demand upon their marriage for things marriage was never intended to do.

Women who place a demand upon their marriage to make them secure and safe can never get what they truly need. They need to know the protection and provision of the Lord. It brings a safety and security that no man on this earth can bring. Once they truly have that, they can allow their husbands to be human, have failures, and not always be everything they want or need. Women are called to be helpmeets to their husbands. Not slaves or servants and not spoiled little girls but women of God who surround their husbands with prayer, support and respect.

When I was remarried, I did not marry my husband because I needed him. I married him because first, I felt that was what the Lord was saying and second, because I wanted to be with him. I didn't get married because I needed someone to take care of me financially. I didn't get married because I was scared to be alone. I didn't get married because I might fall into sexual sin. I didn't get married because I couldn't control my children. I didn't get married because I was lonely. I didn't get married because it was uncomfortable going to social things alone. I didn't get married because I needed someone to fix things, etc. (These are all reasons I have heard before concerning how and why individuals ended up in marriages and relationships that were put together out of the needs of their flesh rather than by the Holy Spirit.) I had already met the one that said, *"Behold, it is I,"* the Lover of my soul, the One who comforted me, provided for me, counseled me, my Healer, my Deliverer, my Redeemer!

After we meet the Lord personally and begin to get to know Him through His Word, then we must begin to know Him through His Body. We need an understanding of spiritual authority that He has placed on the earth, through the family of God, His Church. This next step can be a stumbling block for women who have come out of abusive, destructive relationships with men. They finally say, *"I have met the One who loves me, but now I'm expected to trust you? I'm supposed to trust a pastor, an elder, and people I have relationship with in the church. I don't think so. Men have abused me, used me and cast me off. I can't trust you."* And they go running back to our personal intimate relationship with Jesus. Also, most authority in the church is still predominately male and we have all heard the stories and seen the outcome of men in authority who have abused their power and fallen into sin.

We just have one problem. We are called to be a part of this great community of believers here on the earth. The Lord spoke the following to me when I was dealing with this whole area of wanting a relationship with Him but preferring to stay away from His family, *"People in this day and age who believe they can have a relationship with Me apart from My Body are just as deceived as the Jews who believed they could have a relationship with God apart from their Messiah, Jesus Christ."* God and Jesus are one, when you reject one, you reject the other. Jesus and His Church are one, when you reject one, you reject the other. He comes to us from within His Body and says, *"Behold, it is I."* And we don't recognize Him and run from Him.

GUESS WHAT, HE HAS A FAMILY

Jesus in His grace and mercy allows us to have our intimate relationship with Him for a period of time and then pulls back the cover and says, *"Oh by the way, I'd like you to meet the family."* Like a woman who falls in love with a man and then finds out he has sixteen kids and then wants to run the other way, we try to do everything to continue having a relationship with Jesus apart from His Church. People who demand this type of relationship with the Lord, *"I want to know You but not Your Body,"* end up in a place of immaturity and frustration. They are immature because they have not been discipled. The Word tells us that iron sharpens iron. We need one another. It also tells us that we are joined together and built up together by what each joint supplies. (Ephesians 4:16) They are also frustrated because they have no outlet for their ministry and no place to serve and mature in their gifting.

We must ask the Lord to heal us of our trust issues in order to receive Him through His Body. It's not that we put all of our trust in men and women in leadership and follow them blindly but we trust the Lord enough that He will give us the discernment to know where to submit ourselves. We are actually putting our trust in the Lord over the leadership He places us under. A woman who submits to her husband has to first trust the Lord over Him. She has to trust that God is bigger than her husband and even if he has weaknesses or failures God can keep her in the midst of them.

Now, why is this all so important? Because it is that very leadership and that family of God who will be your protection against the deception of the enemy (if you will let them). They will be the ones saying, *"Don't rush this. I don't have a witness to this. Give him some time and make sure he is really sincere in his Christian walk. This is not God, don't do this."* I'm sure you get the picture. If you do not realize that you are being ministered to by the Lord Himself through His Body, you will reject the counsel and the warnings. Your leadership and your spiritual family will sound the alarm but you will not listen. You will then begin to separate yourself from those relationships so that you can do what it is you are determined to do.

I have personally experienced women leaving the church we pastored after years of fellowship and co-laboring together when we have tried to intervene in a relationship that we felt was out of the timing and will of God. I'm talking about obvious things here. Not just that we didn't feel good about these men. I'm talking about relationships with men who were married and separated from their wives, men who were still having trouble with alcohol, men right out of prison and in the midst of transition with no job, no home, no car, men who had a history of abuse, but refused counseling, etc. When you see it in black and white, you say, *"Surely not."* These true stories are the fuel that has driven me to write this book and sound the alarm.

Deception takes over and one of the protections the Lord has given us is cast off. The safety of a multitude of counsel (Proverbs 15:22) is disregarded. Let me give you a few warning signs:

- *If you have had a friend or have been in fellowship for more than a year with someone and your new relationship causes separation,* **WAKE UP**!
- *If your pastors are not in agreement to a marriage and you decide to have someone else marry you,* **WAKE UP**!
- *If you end up leaving a church because they are not in agreement with your new relationship,* **WAKE UP**!

- *If no one in your natural or spiritual families are supportive of the relationship, **WAKE UP**!*
- *If you feel driven and compulsive in the relationship, **WAKE UP**!*
- *If people are telling you to slow down and examine the fruit of the individual's life and you feel you can't or you won't, **WAKE UP**!*

Is the short term gain of having someone who is giving you some attention, someone who might be easing the loneliness, someone who is making you feel attractive, important enough to put your life back into the prison of an unequally yoked, unhealthy, destructive relationship? These relationships are sent from the pit of hell to cause you to miss destiny. Even if he is the most wonderful guy in the world is he worth missing destiny? Is it worth one day waking up and seeing the friends and family and support no longer there because you had to sacrifice them for the relationship? Is it worth waking up one morning and smelling that familiar smell of vomit and realizing you are covered in it once again?

INTIMACY WITH THE LORD

"Behold, it is I." I encourage you to develop a personal, intimate relationship with the Lord. Know the One who loves you. Only after you really know the Him can you know the one He sends to be that demonstration of His love on the earth. Your husband should be an expression of God's love to you in the flesh. He tells our husbands in Ephesians to love us as Christ loved the Church. I look at some women and see the men they settle for and I have to conclude that they couldn't believe God loved them very much if that was God's best.

Our time in the Word of God, in prayer and worship helps us to develop our intimacy with Him. Intimacy is cultivated through communication and time spent together. It also needs openness and honesty. Religion will not meet those needs, developing a personal relationship with the Lord Jesus Christ will. Religion has us come to God through form and formality. Relationship lets us come with simplicity and realness. When you are in true relationship with the Lord, you never have to worry about being alone again. You never have to worry about long, lonely nights with no one to talk to because He will be there for you. The only time I have ever seen the Lord pulling back on His communication and fellowship with us is when He is determined to have us develop relationship with the rest of His family.

I have ministered to people whom the Lord has ministered to privately hundreds of times and then one day there was something they couldn't get over, couldn't get through, or couldn't get free from unless they got some help. That's the mercy of God that keeps us from independence, spiritual pride and becoming a cancerous cell, doing our own thing, our own way in the Body of Christ.

HEARING THE VOICE OF GOD

Through intimacy and fellowship we develop our ability to hear the voice of the Lord. We were designed and created to know the voice of God. The Bible tells us in John 10:27 that He is a good shepherd and His sheep hear His voice. Before I was saved, I thought people who believed in God were neurotic and were too weak to face life on their own. But the ones who thought God talked to them were psychotic and should just be locked up!

Sometimes we have misconceptions about hearing the voice of God. Many people are still waiting for an audible voice but usually the Lord speaks in that still, small voice within our spirit and speaks to us through our own thoughts. Yet somehow they are different than our normal thoughts. We know that wasn't us, that wasn't our idea or inspiration. To avoid the voice of deception sent from the enemy, we must make sure everything we hear and attribute to God is scriptural. Part of being trained up to hear the Voice of God is to submit what we think we are hearing to those God has put over us and next to us who are more mature, those discipling us in the Lord. Circumcising our spiritual ears also takes time studying the Word. As we study it, we begin to get to know the Lord better and can discern when He is speaking to us.

Sometimes the Lord will speak to us through the peace of God we have in our hearts or the anxiety we experience when it is not Him. He may speak to us through a prophetic dream, a vision, or through an angel. The Lord may speak to us through His prophets, through the gift of prophecy flowing through someone else, or the spirit of prophecy in a corporate anointing. I encourage you to study the Word in relationship to how God has communicated with His people. He is always communicating with us; we just have to get our spirits tuned to the right frequency.

The Lord loves you and wants the best for you, so quit looking for a man and look to Him. When it's His time, He will send the right one handpicked for you – His very best. You may already be in a marriage. Quit looking to it to meet needs God never intended it to provide. Get your eyes on the Lord and trust Him over your husband. Stop nagging, stop complaining, get out of your pity party, get some healing and ministry and turn your natural efforts to change him into spiritual energy. Pray for what needs changing. Become a warrior in the Spirit and take authority over the enemy that is robbing you from the joy of a godly marriage. That may sound simplistic but it really is the only way out. It will take change, effort and discipline on your part. Trust that God loves you enough and is big enough to deal with that husband of yours.

I have heard testimony from women who trusted God over men that were abusive verbally, emotionally and some even physically and the Lord has actually appeared to some of those men in a sovereign way. One woman shared the story of the Lord coming to her husband in his office and basically told him if he didn't start treating her right and supporting her in her ministry, He would physically remove him through death. Needless to say it got his attention and he became a new husband. Put your faith in the Lord and trust Him for the miracle. If there is physical abuse, you may have to separate yourself from the situation for your own safety. Once again, trust the voice of the Lord to lead you. I have heard a number of stories of men who were about to hit a woman and an unseen force restrained them. They were unable to complete the act. Where is your faith? Is it in your ability to nag, to emotionally or sexually manipulate your husband or is it in the grace and power of the Lord Jesus Christ?

The Word tells us that He is the head of man. I always tell women why waste your breath talking to him. Go to his BOSS!

> *Lord, help me to recognize you. Forgive me for not accepting You through Your Church here on earth. Give me a revelation of Your Body and help me to become a part and do my part. Help me to recognize the spiritual authority you place in my life and to allow them to be a voice of safety for me. Forgive me for my independence and my spiritual pride. Circumcise my spiritual ears that I might hear Your Voice. I want to know you, Lord, and I choose to wait upon You and receive Your best for me.*

Chapter 8

Break Forth Into Joy

When I came to this last chapter, I realized that there were a total of eight chapters. The number 8 represents new beginnings. I believe that the Lord is going to give you a new beginning related to this area of your life.

I can tell you from my own experience, the Lord has a new beginning for each and every one of us. And it truly is a new beginning that will cause us to break forth into joy. I can't begin to tell you what a joy it is to know you are in a relationship ordained of the Lord. It is a joy of being cared for rather than being abused; a joy of being fulfilled in a relationship rather than being robbed and cheated.

The Word of God tells us in Jeremiah 31:13 that our mourning will be turned into joy. I have found that the joy of the Lord has increased each year that I have served Him. The joy of having a new life and seeing the restoration of my family is overwhelming. When I came to the Lord as I shared earlier, I had an alcohol problem, I was divorced, I had contracted herpes, I had a man that was stalking me as a result of a relationship I was trying to end and I had more bills than money every month.

The Lord sovereignly delivered me from any desire for alcohol. I was healed of herpes. And I hadn't even gotten to the scripture that said He was the Lord that healed us. I just read the one that said I was a new creature. I decided I needed a new mind because I had burnt so many brain cells with alcohol. I needed a new heart because the old one had been broken too many times. And I needed a new body because of the herpes. I repented from my sexual immorality because I knew that was the open door and asked the Lord to take it away. A couple of years after the Lord healed me the thought crossed my mind that the herpes might just be in remission. And just as quick, I heard the voice of the Lord saying, *"Daughter your faith has made you whole."* I have a wonderful marriage and the Lord has prospered us naturally and spiritually. Yes, I can break forth into joy.

Have there been ups and downs, heartaches and the testing of the Lord? Yes, but through it all He has been faithful. The Word of God tells us in Nehemiah that the joy of the Lord is our strength. As you discover the truth of the joy of the Lord, you find that it is something that raises you above your circumstances. Happiness comes out of your circumstances. Joy is not dependent on your circumstances; it is dependent on your relationship with your Savior.

It reminds me of a lesson I learned a number of years ago. I had gotten up, and it was a beautiful day. The sun was shining. Nothing bad was happening in my life. I was feeling good and I walked to the mail box singing and praising the Lord. When I opened my mail on my walk back, I discovered a very negative piece of mail. Everything drained out of me, I was very upset. But in the midst of it the Lord spoke to me and said, "You *thought you had the joy of the Lord didn't you?*" I agreed, *"Yes."* And He said, *"No, you didn't, it doesn't go away that easily, you had the joy of the day. The sun was shining, the birds were singing, and it made you feel good."* I realized then that I really didn't know the true meaning of the joy of the Lord. I went to the Word of God and did a study on it. I encourage you to do the same thing. Where does joy come from? Why do we need it? How do we lose it? How do we keep it? Ask the Holy Spirit to be your teacher and teach you about true joy.

HOW TO GET THE LORD TO COME TO YOUR HOUSE

The joy of the Lord will allow you to praise and worship even if everything is not perfect in your life. I remember being in a service and nothing was going the way I wanted it to or thought it should. I didn't feel like praising God. The people around me were even irritating me as they praised the Lord. Have you ever been there? Yet, I knew I had to be obedient and praise the Lord despite what my flesh was trying to dictate. I began to praise out of obedience until it got in my spirit. About six months later, I was back in the same church, everything in my life had undergone change – change that I was excited about! I really wanted to praise the Lord. As I started worshipping, the Lord reminded me of the time I had been in the same church without being in the mood to praise Him. And He told me that if I hadn't praised Him by faith then, I would not have had anything to praise Him about now. It was my obedience and faith that unlocked the door to prayer being answered in my life. The Lord *inhabits* the praises of His people. If He hasn't been showing up at your house, you may not be giving Him a habitation.

We are coming to the close of our journey. I want you to know that even though I have said some hard things to help wake you up and shake you, my heart goes out to you. I know you don't want to end up in unhealthy relationships or live in bad marriages. As I said earlier, I have tasted the pain first hand. I know the road out isn't always easy, but I know there is a road out.

Won't you taste and see that the Lord is good? Living life according to His Ways and His Word will begin to produce the Kingdom of God in your life and the Word tells us that the Kingdom is righteousness, peace and joy in the Holy Ghost. (Romans 14:17)

RED LIGHT – GREEN LIGHT

I want to encourage you to get a support system if you don't have one. Get plugged into a good local church and become accountable to the leadership there. Quit dating if you're single. Dating is just rehearsal for divorce. You date and break up, date and break up. Wait until you find someone that you feel the Lord is serious about, pray about the relationship; ask your support system to pray about it. When there are green lights, then proceed into courtship. If there is a yellow light, wait on the timing of the Lord, slow down. And if there is a red light, stay away; it could be dangerous to your destiny.

I would encourage you to go to your local Christian book store and read some books related to courtship versus dating. Dating is an unbiblical practice. That is why there are no scriptural guidelines that can help us with the process. Courtship is the agreement of families, authority, and the individuals involved that the Lord is approving of a relationship that will end in marriage. You may not be 100% sure when you enter into courtship but you should be 95% or more sure. It should not be entered into lightly. In the meantime, deepen your relationship with the Lord, with your church body, with family and friends and prepare yourself by allowing the Lord to heal areas in your life and equip you for a relationship. Trust me, it is worth the wait. Dating creates soul ties which can actually lead to marriage just because people get comfortable with the other person. They care about them and don't want to hurt them. Those reasons just aren't enough to sustain a marriage relationship.

Marriage was a God idea. He instituted the institution of marriage. If it was that important to God, He must have a special plan for our marriages. And if He has a special plan for us, He has a special man for us. Wait on the Lord, it's worth it.

If you are already in a marriage, learn how to set healthy boundaries so you are not abused. Get help and support from a counselor or a minister. Don't accept less. Pray and begin to war in the spirit realm. The Word of God tells us in Ephesians 6:12 that we do not fight against flesh and blood but against principalities and powers and wickedness in high places. Quit fighting with your husband in the natural; it doesn't do any good. The Lord knows the position you are in, start praying and asking the Lord for a new husband. Now, I didn't say a different husband. I said a new one. If the Lord can make people new creatures through salvation, He can make your husband a new man but first He wants to make you a new woman, a woman who values herself, a woman whose mind has been renewed to what God says about her, a woman who knows she deserves to be treated with respect and loving care.

I want you to know I love you and I stand in the gap and intercede so that you can be set free from the bondage of unhealthy relationships:

Lord, I pray for _____ *(your name) and I ask you to surround her with Your love and Your acceptance. I pray that you would keep her set aside for the special man that you have chosen for her. Lord, if she is married, I pray that you would make her husband a new man. Change him, Lord. And I pray that you would give* _____ *the grace and patience to hold on through the process. Lord, help her to forgive every man that has ever wronged her. Turn her mourning into joy. Give her a new beginning I bless you in the Name of Jesus and agree with you for victory in this area of your life. Amen* (which actually means, *"so be it."*)

One New Women Enters The Gates Of Heaven

By Victoria Gambino

*One New Woman, accepted, respected, cherished and loved
knows who she is in Christ, and is loyal to the Lord above.*

*She's directed and receives truth in her inward parts
She's unveiled, transparent, and submitted to God.*

*He's made her a Godly woman with the Mind of Christ
She's dependent on God for a pure and peaceful life.*

*She's empowered by God, thankful and full of hope
An encourager with the ability to say no.*

*She's an overcomer, secure and saved.
Resting in the Lord, her womanhood's embraced.*

*She has the spirit of excellence, healthy boundaries are made.
She is able to receive the joy and blessings God gave.*

*God is the provider.
He's healed the things inside her.*

*She is forgiving and merciful,
has respect for men, and knows they are equal.*

*Releasing situations and people to God; she's relaxed, slim, and healthy
One New Woman, with no facade.*

WEBSTER: Fa`cade - an imposing appearance concealing something inferior.

MORE BY THIS AUTHOR

Restoring Sexuality
Soul Battles
Birth Assignments
Straight Talk
Prodigal Daughter (1st Novel in Trilogy)
Redeemed (2nd Novel in Trilogy)
Legacy "The Torch Bearers" (3rd Novel in Trilogy – Coming Soon)

to order contact: info@kingdomlifenow.com
www.KingdomLifeNow.com

Made in the USA
San Bernardino, CA
23 September 2015